# THE HOW AND WHY WONDER BOOK OF

# TIME

Written by GENE LIBERTY

Illustrated by JO KOTULA

Editorial Production: DONALD D. WOLF

Edited under the supervision of
Dr. Paul E. Blackwood
Washington, D. C.

Text and illustrations approved by
Oakes A. White
Brooklyn Children's Museum,
Brooklyn, New York

GROSSET & DUNLAP·Publishers·NEW YORK

# Introduction

What is time? Time is something elusive which is at the center of our day to day activities. Sometimes we say time flies; sometimes we say it drags. We cannot see time or feel it or hear it. But we can measure it.

Time, it has been said, is the interval between events. To measure time you must select regularly occuring events and then devise ways of measuring the intervals between their occurrence and reoccurrence. *The How and Why Wonder Book of Time* tells of man's search through the ages for practical ways of measuring these intervals. This book also tells how time is important to each of us and particularly to scientists in their unending quest for new knowledge about the universe.

The inventiveness of people is demonstrated by the many kinds of clocks that have been developed. Do you know how a burning rope or a water clock or a molecular clock tells time? Could you make a sundial, a candle clock or a sand glass? *The How and Why Wonder Book of Time* answers these questions and many more, and also gives you instructions for making your own clocks. This book, studied at home and in school, will enlighten young readers about many fascinating aspects of man's preoccupation with the "interval between events."

*Paul E. Blackwood*

Dr. Blackwood is a professional employee in the U. S. Office of Education. This book was edited by him in his private capacity and no official support or endorsement by the Office of Education is intended or should be inferred.

Library of Congress Catalog Card Number: 63-16317

# Contents

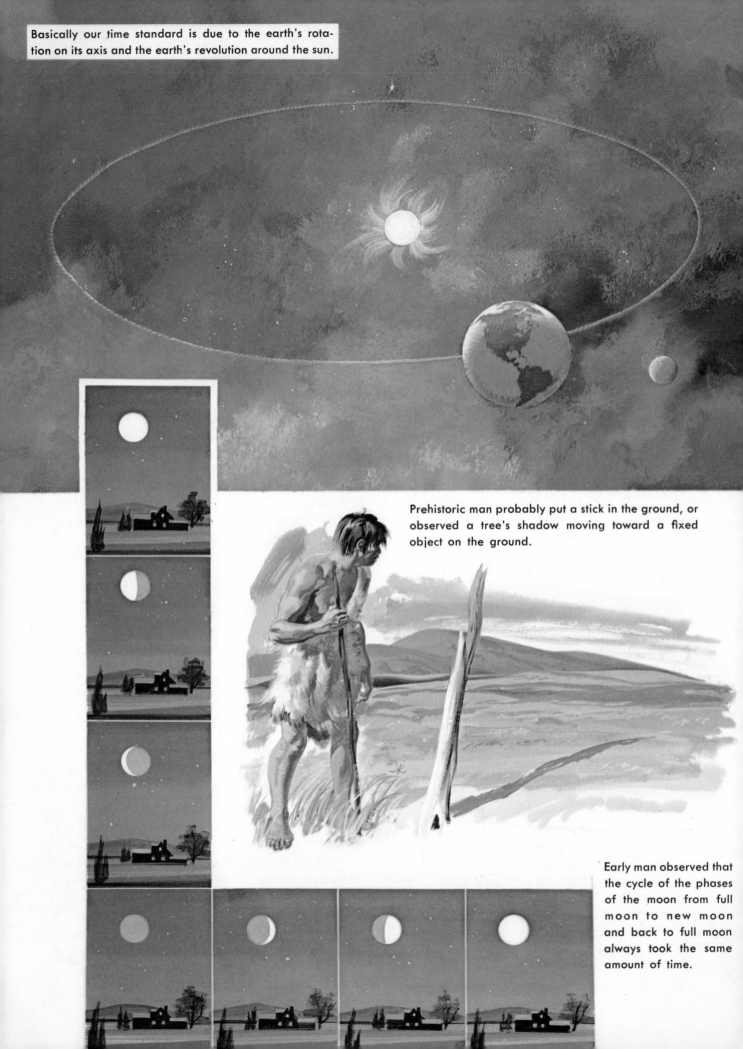

Basically our time standard is due to the earth's rotation on its axis and the earth's revolution around the sun.

Prehistoric man probably put a stick in the ground, or observed a tree's shadow moving toward a fixed object on the ground.

Early man observed that the cycle of the phases of the moon from full moon to new moon and back to full moon always took the same amount of time.

# Seconds and Centuries

Time is measured by the journey of our planet through space. The earth's yearly trip around the sun, the monthly orbit of the moon, and the daily rotation of the earth on its axis give us a standard for the length of the year, the month and the day. Like gravity and the atom, time is one of the great natural phenomena that we are learning to explore and understand.

Time has a quality that is as hazy and distant as a night sky before rain. The haze occasionally clears for one of our scientists or poets, and through them a glimpse of the structure or meaning of time is revealed.

Although our knowledge of time is growing, and we can accurately measure its passage, time itself remains aloof from our control. Men have never been able to change time. It is time that has permitted men to see change.

**How did men first tell time?** Primitive man responded to the passing of time only as it paced the span of his survival. Daylight was a period for him to hunt food, and darkness allowed rest. He knew the overall seasonal rhythms — when they brought different periods of night and day, extremes of hot and cold, and a shift in the bounty of game and plant food. Ul-

A large circle of monoliths or very large stones stands at Stonehenge, in England. For many centuries no one really knew where the stones came from and for what purpose they were put there. Today some scholars think that Stonehenge was a "calendar for one day." This day was about June 22, the summer solstice (the longest day of the year) 4000 years ago. The heel stone, slaughter stone and altar stone were apparently arranged so that they pointed toward the rising sun only on this day.

5

timately the growth of his children and the aging of his body revealed to him that he had lived through a great many night-and-day cycles and seasonal changes. Years were accumulating.

As the human race evolved, tribes became organized. There was a need to coordinate hunting parties, councils and religious ceremonies. When do we meet, when do we talk, when do we appeal to our gods? A measurement of time that everybody could use was required, and somewhere back in our history, long before the ages of metal or the written record, time-telling started.

The measurement of time probably began with observations based on the movements of the sun and the moon. The rising and setting of the sun marked the day. In the evenings, ceremonies arranged to start when the moon was full or partly visible, gave men a broader measure of time.

In the interval from full moon to full moon, approximately 29½ days were counted. Then men began to record these moon-months and discovered that 12 of them added up to a full cycle of the four seasons. The arithmetic of our own calendar was slowly developing.

Shadows cast by the changing position of the sun are one of the simplest ways to measure the day. Men observed that morning and evening shadows were the longest and that at noon, when the sun is overhead, the shadow is the shortest. The first sundials were trees and rocks and then, perhaps, a straight branch set in the center of a circle of rocks. Hours were as yet unknown, but men had learned to divide the time between sunrise and sunset into smaller periods.

**What do shadows tell us about time?**

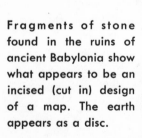

Fragments of stone found in the ruins of ancient Babylonia show what appears to be an incised (cut in) design of a map. The earth appears as a disc.

The astronomer-priests of Babylonia were keen observers of the stars and had a broad knowledge of astronomy. ▶

# Calendars Old and New

Over many thousands of years, primitive ways of life gradually were replaced by the development of civilization. Cities took form, learning and knowledge increased in importance, trade reached to far areas, and skilled crafts multiplied. Life became more complicated and men began to seek better ways of telling time to guide their activities.

One of the first great advances in time telling was the **Who were the time tellers of Babylon?** remarkable lunar (moon) calendar of the ancient Babylonians. The study of the heavens among these people of the Euphrates Valley was carried on by the astronomer-priests, who blended superstition with brilliant astronomy.

Religious prophecy and guidance proved to be profitable occupations among an uneducated people. The astronomer-priests manipulated their star charts to bring them wealth and political authority. Yet much of their science of the skies, achieved without telescopes or fine instruments, was so practical and reliable that we still use it today.

The astronomer-priests carefully separated the heavens into a giant circular band of 12 equal distances called the *zodiac*. Each distance was identified by a constellation, or cluster of stars, that served as a signpost to point out the route of the sun as it seemed to pass from one constellation to the next.

Actually the astronomer-priests did not know that it was the movement of

A Babylonian stone cutter makes a "calendar" based on the observations of the moon by the astronomers.

7

the earth that made the sun appear to be in motion. Unlike the passenger who realizes that it is actually his train that is moving when the landscape seems to rush past, the astronomer-priests were deceived by our inability to see the earth move.

The sun took one year to complete its apparent cycle through the 12 sections of the zodiac. The solar year was divided into 12

**Why do we have twelve months?**

parts. There were now 12 divisions of the year, each an interval of time matching the 12 zodiac measurements of distance.

The time it took for the sun to travel between two constellations of the zodiac also roughly equalled the time required by the moon to complete all of its phases. Both durations of time were what we now call a month. With the two heavenly bodies in agreement, the year became 360 days of 12 equal months, each month containing 30 days.

The zodiac is still used by astronomers to map the skies and also by present day astrologers, who have kept alive the heavenly superstitions of the Babylonian priests. They use the zodiac signs to predict the future of human affairs. In current English, words like *saturnine, moon-struck, ill-starred, lunatic* and *capricious* are part of the superstitious inheritance of astrology.

The Babylonian astronomer-priests divided space as well as time.

Names and figures designating the constellations of the zodiac are still the same. The inner band shows the Greek signs which we still use today. ▶

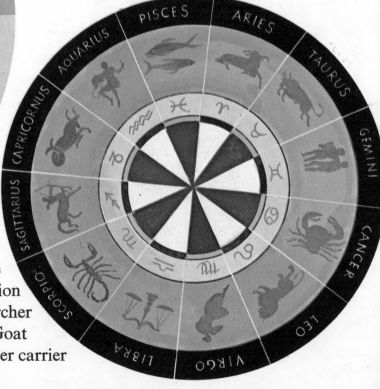

### THE TWELVE CONSTELLATIONS OF THE ZODIAC

Aries, the Ram  
Taurus, the Bull  
Gemini, the Twins  
Cancer, the Crab  
Leo, the Lion  
Virgo, the Virgin  

Libra, the Balance  
Scorpio, the Scorpion  
Sagittarius, the Archer  
Capricornus, the Goat  
Aquarius, the Water carrier  
Pisces, the Fishes

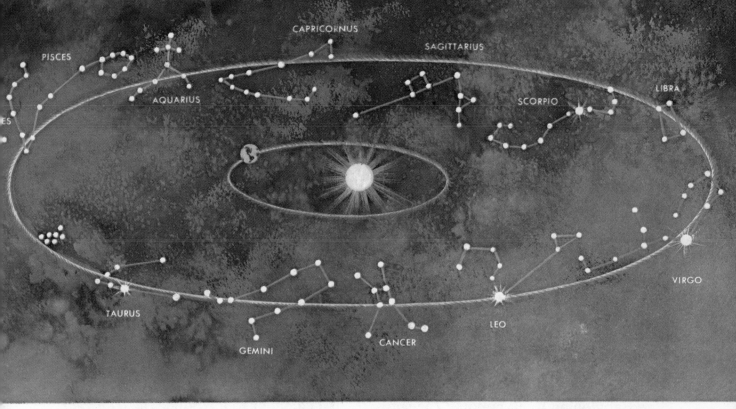

The diagram above shows the sun (center), the earth and its orbit, and the apparent circle the constellations of the zodiac seem to make around the solar system.

The Babylonians used the number 60

**What is unusual about the number sixty?**

for the standard of measure in both civil affairs and astronomy. Although 60 was a mystic number, it was as important to science as it was to religion. Sixty has great versatility because it can be divided by more numbers than any other lower number. This ease of division made 60 an excellent choice for scientific measurement.

Day and night were each assigned 12 hours in recognition of the power of the zodiac. The number of minutes in an hour was then set at 60, and each minute was subdivided into 60 seconds. If you look at your watch, you will see how naturally 5 minute periods, quarter-hours and half-hours are divided. Combinations like 10, 20 or 40 minutes are revealed at a glance.

The astronomer-priests divided space as well as time. They split the circle into 360 degrees. Each degree had 60 minutes, and each minute had 60 seconds.

The week and the hour are inventions of

**Could we have a twenty or a forty hour day?**

superstition and convenience. The day, the month and the year depend on the movement of bodies in space, but the week and the hour are artificial measurements that help us to organize our own activities without any direction from nature. We probably could live just as comfortably if our day were divided into 20 or 40 units and our week into 6 or 8 units. But 24 hours and 7 days are the units that have been with us a long time, and a change to new units is unlikely. The ancient Scandinavians, however, had a 5 day week, and some tribes in Africa still use weeks of 3, 4, 5, 6 and 8 days.

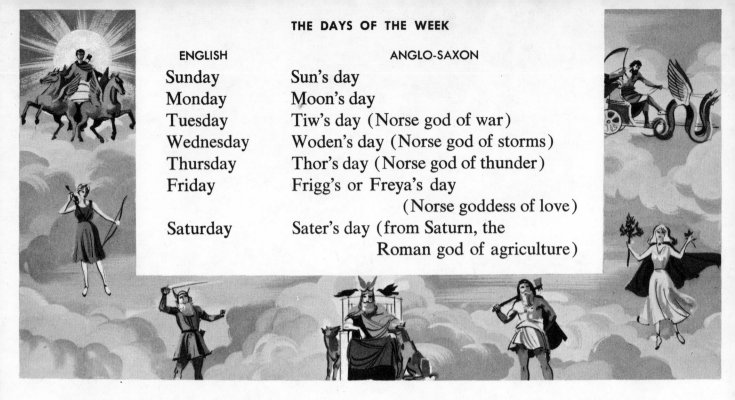

## THE DAYS OF THE WEEK

| ENGLISH | ANGLO-SAXON |
|---|---|
| Sunday | Sun's day |
| Monday | Moon's day |
| Tuesday | Tiw's day (Norse god of war) |
| Wednesday | Woden's day (Norse god of storms) |
| Thursday | Thor's day (Norse god of thunder) |
| Friday | Frigg's or Freya's day (Norse goddess of love) |
| Saturday | Sater's day (from Saturn, the Roman god of agriculture) |

The Babylonian week honored the sun, the moon and the 5 planets that were known at the time.

**How were the days named?**

Each day was intended for the worship of a different heavenly body. Other people later dedicated the days to other gods, and although their religious significance is gone, the ancient names of the days are not lost. They have passed through many languages and are retained in modern English.

The astronomer-priests soon discovered that their 12 month year of 360 days was too short.

**Why do we have leap years?**

The error of approximately 5 days per year accumulated quickly: in the brief time of 6 years a full month of 30 days was lost. They partially overcame this deficiency by adding a thirteenth month to the sixth year. The corrected calendar now contained 5 consecutive 12 month years followed by 1 year with 13 months. This was the first calendar to introduce the *leap year*. A leap year is any year which has an extra day or days added to it in order to compensate for shortages in the calendar.

It is also the year when the ladies traditionally abandon their gentle manner and cheerfully chase after eligible gentlemen with proposals of marriage. Today leap-year husbands are humorously regarded as victims of unofficial custom, but the rules for catching a bachelor with the help of the calendar were once written into the laws of some countries.

One of the earliest of these laws, which many historians believe is an amusing myth, was supposed to have been enacted in Scotland in 1288: "It is stated and ordained that during the rein (rule) of his most blessed Majesty, for every yeare known as lepe yeare, every maiden ladye of both high and low rank shall have liberty to propose to the man she likes, should he refuse to take her to be his lawful wyfe, he

The chase is on: leap year 1288 in Scotland, legally sanctioned.

shall be fined for the sum of one pound or less, befitting his rank; except and always if he can make it appear that he is betrothed to another woman he then shall be free."

In Egypt, the priests were also gifted astronomers. It is difficult to establish the exact date of the first Egyptian calendar, but some historians agree that it was 4241 B.C. This date is sometimes called the oldest recorded year in history. Starting with a 12 month year of 360 days, the Egyptians eventually learned that they needed more days to complete the year. Five feast days were added to the end of the year; however, the new

**Why did Egypt ignore the leap year?**

Houses of worship in Egypt were used not only for religious purposes. They were also used as observatories for the sun and stars. At Karnak, for instance, the temple had a row of columns pointing to the rising sun at midsummer's day. Only once in 365 days did the sun's rays shine straight along that line.

The Egyptian pyramids or tombs, shown on page 13, were used at the same time by the priests for sighting stars. Priests pinpointed the position of certain stars in relation to a fixed object.

Above, Sirius the Dog Star in the constellation of the Greater Dog.

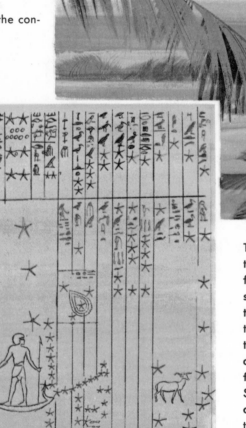

The Egyptian astronomer-priests observed that flooding of the Nile, so vital for the fertility of the soil, took place every year soon after the day the brightest star, Sirius the Dog Star, appeared before sunrise in the sky. This day was the ancient Egyptian's New Year's day. On the ceiling of an Egyptian tomb, archaeologists have found paintings that show the positions of Sirius, depicted as a god, and records of observations pertaining to Sirius' orbit in the year 2035 B.C. At left, a detail from this ceiling; above, Nile landscape shortly before the rising of the waters.

calendar of 365 days was still inaccurate. A true solar year (the time it takes the earth to travel around the sun) measures close to 365¼ days. The Egyptian calendar, like the Babylonian, slowly drifted away from the seasons, losing one quarter of a day each year.

In 238 B. C. Ptolemy III, the ruler of Egypt, attempted to regain the lost quarter of a day by inserting into the calendar one day every 4 years. His leap year amendment was not accepted by the priests, who refused to alter the routine of religious observances which depended on the calendar. Almost 200 years after it was rejected in his

own country, Ptolemy's leap year was adopted by Julius Caesar. The Roman emperor developed a calendar that was to become the standard of the Western world for over 1600 years.

Up to the time of Julius Caesar, the Romans used a calendar that was irregular and confusing.

**How was the calendar abused by Roman officials?**

Months were shortened or lengthened for political purposes, so that officials could vary their terms of office to accommodate favorable schemes. The calendar was changed so many times

and had fallen so far behind, that it became impossible to plan the details of civil administration or trade.

Reform was necessary and Caesar turned to the Greek astronomer Sosigenes for advice. The two men decided to replace the old Roman calendar with

An old Roman stone calendar-almanac of the first century A.D. had three months on each of its four sides. The front slab carries information and advice covering the months of January, February and March.

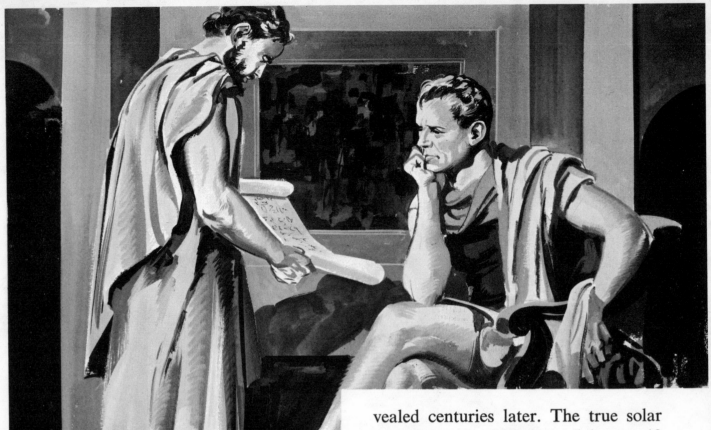

The calendar invented by Julius Caesar and Sosigenes was used by the Western world from 45 B.C. until 1582 A.D.

an altered version of the solar calendar of the Egyptians.

The 5 additional days placed at the end of the Egyptian year were abolished, and each year was assigned 365 calendar days. But as the actual length of the year was approximately one quarter day longer than 365 days, Caesar decreed that every fourth year should be a leap year of 366 days. The extra day of the leap year was added to the shortest month, February.

The Julian calendar, named after Julius

**What was wrong with the Julian Calendar?**

Caesar, was inaugurated January 1, 45 B.C. Although it was a bold and successful calendar that was superior to its predecessors, an error was re-

vealed centuries later. The true solar year measures 365 days, 5 hours, 48 minutes and 46 seconds, a figure that is 11 minutes and 14 seconds less than the 365¼ days used by Caesar and Sosigenes. Because the Roman year was slightly longer than the solar year, the practice of adding a day to the fourth year introduced an error of about 3 days every 400 years.

In ancient Rome all months except February had either 29 or 31 days because odd numbers were considered lucky. The end of the year was thought to be unlucky, and February was made the shortest month and given an even 28 days. This tradition partly influenced the scientific reform of Caesar. He assigned 31 days to seven of the months; 30 days, an unlucky even number, to four of the months; and retained the short length of 28 days for February. The names of the months that we use today are derived from the ancient Roman names.

**JANUARY**
(31 days)

From the double-faced Roman god *Janus,* whose two faces looked into both the past and future. He influenced the beginnings of all undertakings and was honored by receiving the name of the first month of the year.

**FEBRUARY**
(28 or 29 days)

From *Februa,* a Roman festival of purification, held on February 15.

**MARCH**
(31 days)

From *Mars,* the Roman god of war. The Anglo-Saxons called March the "lengthening month" because the days grow longer.

**APRIL**
(30 days)

Exact derivation is uncertain. April may have come from the Latin verb "to open," *aperire,* a reference to the sprouting or opening of vegetation in the spring.

**MAY**
(31 days)

From *Maia,* the Roman goddess of growth.

**JUNE**
(30 days)

Exact derivation is uncertain. One possibility is that June was named for *Juno,* the Roman goddess who was queen of heaven; it also could have come from the name *Junius.*

**JULY**
(31 days)

Named for Julius Caesar, who was born in the month of July.

**AUGUST**
(31 days)

Named for the Roman emperor Octavius Augustus because of his many victories in this month.

**SEPTEMBER**
(30 days)

From the Latin *septem,* meaning seven. In the old Roman calendar, September was the seventh month. The Swiss call September *Herbstmonat,* the month of harvest.

**OCTOBER**
(31 days)

From the Latin *octo,* meaning eight. The Slavs called October the "yellow month" to describe the time of year when leaves turn yellow.

**NOVEMBER**
(30 days)

From the Latin *novem,* meaning nine. The "wind month" and the "blood month" were Anglo-Saxon names for November.

**DECEMBER**
(31 days)

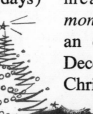

From the Latin *decem,* meaning ten. *Helighmonath* (holy month) is an old Saxon name for December, the month of Christmas.

Caesar left a valuable bequest to calendar science, but his calendar could not outlive its errors. A change was needed. This time it was a religious group that produced the next great calendar reform.

Catholic officials were disturbed to find

**How did a "wandering holiday" give us our present calendar?**

that the errors in the Julian calendar would ultimately cause Easter to arrive in the winter. Easter is traditionally celebrated in the spring, and religious leaders wanted to perpetuate the tradition.

For hundreds of years unsuccessful appeals for a new calendar had been made to rulers and popes. Finally Pope Gregory XIII decided to give his attention to the problem of the date of Easter. In the year 1582 A.D., Gregory, assisted by a council of scientists, stabilized the calendar to within 26 seconds of the solar year — a loss of only one day in 3,323 years.

This accuracy was achieved with a new leap year rule that affects the century years. Century years are those years that end with a double zero, for example, 1800 and 1900. The Pope and his council ordered that no century year could be a leap year unless it was divisible by 400. Thus 1600, 2000 and 2400 are leap years, but 1700, 1800 and 1900 are regular years. All other years adhere to the four year rule (one 366 day every four years) of the Julian calendar. The omission of 3 leap year days out of every 400 years was the simple formula that retired the Julian calendar.

The Gregorian calendar, which we use

**Was Gregory's calendar accepted by the world?**

today, was quickly installed in Spain, Portugal, France, parts of Italy and the Catholic states of Germany. The Protestant countries of Sweden and Denmark and the Protestant states of Germany accepted the Gregorian calendar in 1700. Great Britain and the American Colonies made the change in 1752, Japan in 1873 and China in 1912. Russia adopted the Gregorian calendar in 1918 but later abandoned it to experiment with some original calendars. Five and six day weeks were tried but these were not too successful, and in 1940 Russia returned to the Gregorian system.

The calendar that Gregory modified and passed on to us resembles a history book with pages that mix narratives of science, religion, pagan legends and the private politics of ancient civilizations.

Although some of the history of time measurement is too old and dim to be read easily, two contributions stand out as the clearest influences on our calendar.

The first of these was the inspired solar calendars of the Babylonians and Egyptians. Theirs was perhaps the greatest achievement of calendar science, for it created a dependable system of time measurement that regulated human activities to the seasons.

Our second direct link between the calendar and the

**Why do we observe a Sabbath?**

past gives us one of the patterns of modern life — the weekly observance

The French Revolution swept away many old traditions. The calendar was discarded along with Sundays, royalty and religious festivals. The new calendar had different names for the months and the days, and started with 1792 to commemorate the year of French liberty. After a few years, however, the international Gregorian Calendar was restored.

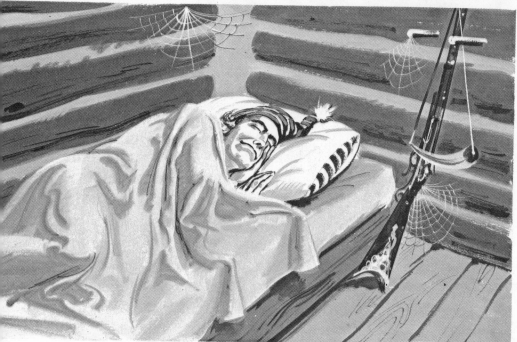

The longest night in American history occured on September 2, 1752. During the change-over from the Julian to the Gregorian Calendar, 11 days were lost. Americans who went to bed on the night of Sept. 2 woke up on the morning of September 14.

The Julian Calendar is still used by the Greek and Russian Churches. People of these faiths celebrate Christmas after the Catholic and Protestant festivals.

The ruins of the observatory of Chichen Itza in Yucatan, Mexico, once the center of the second Mayan empire.

The Mayans, had a sun calendar, and used special numerals shaped like human faces for their records of dates. These were carved on stone columns called steles.

of a Sabbath. Historically this is the dedication, which we still observe, of the seventh day of the week for rest and worship. Sabbath comes from the Hebrew *shabbat,* meaning a day of rest. The Jews perpetuated this custom in order to develop a better way of life rather than for scientific reasons.

The tradition of the Sabbath was not formally blessed until the proclamation of the holiness of the seventh day in the Ten Commandments.

The ancient Jewish calendar, in which the day begins at sunset, is used by the government of Israel and by Jews everywhere for religious purposes. Months are calculated by the moon, and the sun determines the year. The first year is reckoned from the traditional Creation, 3761 B.C., and the New Year generally arrives in September. Varying from 353 to 385 days, the Jewish year contains 12 months of 29 to 30 days each and is kept up to date by inserting a 13th month 7 times during every 19 year period.

The Moslem calendar is even more confusing than the Jewish. "Twelve months is the number of months ordained by God, according to God," is the verse of the Koran that established the Moslem cal-

**Why is the Moslem Calendar confusing?**

cycles of 60, similar to our week that uses a cycle of 7 days.

In India there are close to thirty different calendars, some of which are based on the sun and the moon, while others rely on religious doctrines and astrology. The muddle caused by the hodgepodge of competing calendars has stirred many Indian leaders to work for a simpler system. Since 1957 the government has officially recommended that only two calendars be used — the Gregorian and a new national calendar.

The Aztec calendar was similar to, but not as accurate as the one used by the Mayas. Above, an Aztec calendar stone — a 50 ton monolith found in Mexico in 1790. Its hieroglyphic writing is still not completely deciphered.

endar. These words were taken from a proclamation of Mohammed, and his followers analyzed the Prophet's intent in a strict manner.

They created a completely lunar calendar that ignores the sun and allows the months to wander without regard to the seasons. For example, one year the month of *Rajab* may be a winter month, but several years later it will appear in the summer. For trade or international exchange, however, Moslems now use the Gregorian calendar, and many of their newspapers are double-dated.

The Chinese also live with two calendars: the

**How are some Oriental Calendars arranged?**

*Hsi-li,* or Gregorian Calendar, and the ancient (2397 B.C.) Chinese calendar in which dates are given by naming the day, the moon and the year. The days are grouped into

The sciences of astronomy and mathematics still have not been accepted

**What was the Mayan Calendar like?**

everywhere in the modern world as the basis for time charts. Perhaps this is why we are awed when we look back 2000 years at a primitive people like the Mayan Indians of Mexico and Guatemala, who, without the tools of our advanced science, were able to develop a remarkable calendar of 365.24 days.

The Mayan year of 365 days was divided into 18 months of 20 days each, to which were added 5 days. They used a period of 52 years for a larger unit of time that was comparable to our century. Corrections were introduced as required, and despite the cumbersome system of numbers, the symmetry and order of the calendar were maintained.

Not much is known about the Mayan system of astronomy. But for its time it must have been superlative; these people accurately determined the orbit of Venus who was worshipped as their most important god, after the sun.

Many improvements have been suggested to eliminate the inconsistencies

**Would you prefer the World Calendar?**

that still exist in our present Gregorian calendar. From one year to the next, new calendars have to be printed. National events, holidays, birthdays, rent and insurance payments, pay days and all of the business and recreation of our lively society never fall on the same day. One reform, called the World Calendar, uses the same calendar every year and is designed with simplicity and arithmetical precision. The year is divided into 4 equal quarters of 13 weeks each and each quarter begins on a Sunday and ends on a Saturday. There are 364 numbered days in the year, and every month

has 26 weekdays instead of the 24 to 27 that we now have.

The 365th day, placed after December 30, is called Worldsday and is intended as an international holiday to affirm the bond that exists between all people. In leap years, the extra day is added to the end of June.

At the beginning of the new year the exact cycle is repeated, and corresponding dates occur on the same day every year. To illustrate: June 3, whether the year is 1965, 1987 or any year selected at random, will always be a Sunday. Every year, Christmas, December 25, would fall on a Monday and allow a long weekend.

A number of world leaders and scientists have endorsed the World Calendar as a stable system of time measurement. But like many other worthwhile reforms, before the World Calendar can be universally adopted, it will have to overcome tradition and prejudice.

| JANUARY | | | | | | |
|---|---|---|---|---|---|---|
| S | M | T | W | T | F | S |
| 1 | 2 | 3 | 4 | 5 | 6 | 7 |
| 8 | 9 | 10 | 11 | 12 | 13 | 14 |
| 15 | 16 | 17 | 18 | 19 | 20 | 21 |
| 22 | 23 | 24 | 25 | 26 | 27 | 28 |
| 29 | 30 | 31 | | | | |

| FEBRUARY | | | | | | |
|---|---|---|---|---|---|---|
| S | M | T | W | T | F | S |
| | | | | 1 | 2 | 3 | 4 |
| 5 | 6 | 7 | 8 | 9 | 10 | 11 |
| 12 | 13 | 14 | 15 | 16 | 17 | 18 |
| 19 | 20 | 21 | 22 | 23 | 24 | 25 |
| 26 | 27 | 28 | 29 | 30 | | |

| MARCH | | | | | | |
|---|---|---|---|---|---|---|
| S | M | T | W | T | F | S |
| | | | | | 1 | 2 |
| 3 | 4 | 5 | 6 | 7 | 8 | 9 |
| 10 | 11 | 12 | 13 | 14 | 15 | 16 |
| 17 | 18 | 19 | 20 | 21 | 22 | 23 |
| 24 | 25 | 26 | 27 | 28 | 29 | 30 |

| APRIL | | | | | | |
|---|---|---|---|---|---|---|
| S | M | T | W | T | F | S |
| 1 | 2 | 3 | 4 | 5 | 6 | 7 |
| 8 | 9 | 10 | 11 | 12 | 13 | 14 |
| 15 | 16 | 17 | 18 | 19 | 20 | 21 |
| 22 | 23 | 24 | 25 | 26 | 27 | 28 |
| 29 | 30 | 31 | | | | |

| MAY | | | | | | |
|---|---|---|---|---|---|---|
| S | M | T | W | T | F | S |
| | | | | 1 | 2 | 3 | 4 |
| 5 | 6 | 7 | 8 | 9 | 10 | 11 |
| 12 | 13 | 14 | 15 | 16 | 17 | 18 |
| 19 | 20 | 21 | 22 | 23 | 24 | 25 |
| 26 | 27 | 28 | 29 | 30 | | |

| JUNE | | | | | | |
|---|---|---|---|---|---|---|
| S | M | T | W | T | F | S |
| | | | | | 1 | 2 |
| 3 | 4 | 5 | 6 | 7 | 8 | 9 |
| 10 | 11 | 12 | 13 | 14 | 15 | 16 |
| 17 | 18 | 19 | 20 | 21 | 22 | 23 |
| 24 | 25 | 26 | 27 | 28 | 29 | 30 |

| JULY | | | | | | |
|---|---|---|---|---|---|---|
| S | M | T | W | T | F | S |
| 1 | 2 | 3 | 4 | 5 | 6 | 7 |
| 8 | 9 | 10 | 11 | 12 | 13 | 14 |
| 15 | 16 | 17 | 18 | 19 | 20 | 21 |
| 22 | 23 | 24 | 25 | 26 | 27 | 28 |
| 29 | 30 | 31 | | | | |

| AUGUST | | | | | | |
|---|---|---|---|---|---|---|
| S | M | T | W | T | F | S |
| | | | | 1 | 2 | 3 | 4 |
| 5 | 6 | 7 | 8 | 9 | 10 | 11 |
| 12 | 13 | 14 | 15 | 16 | 17 | 18 |
| 19 | 20 | 21 | 22 | 23 | 24 | 25 |
| 26 | 27 | 28 | 29 | 30 | | |

| SEPTEMBER | | | | | | |
|---|---|---|---|---|---|---|
| S | M | T | W | T | F | S |
| | | | | | 1 | 2 |
| 3 | 4 | 5 | 6 | 7 | 8 | 9 |
| 10 | 11 | 12 | 13 | 14 | 15 | 16 |
| 17 | 18 | 19 | 20 | 21 | 22 | 23 |
| 24 | 25 | 26 | 27 | 28 | 29 | 30 |

| OCTOBER | | | | | | |
|---|---|---|---|---|---|---|
| S | M | T | W | T | F | S |
| 1 | 2 | 3 | 4 | 5 | 6 | 7 |
| 8 | 9 | 10 | 11 | 12 | 13 | 14 |
| 15 | 16 | 17 | 18 | 19 | 20 | 21 |
| 22 | 23 | 24 | 25 | 26 | 27 | 28 |
| 29 | 30 | 31 | | | | |

| NOVEMBER | | | | | | |
|---|---|---|---|---|---|---|
| S | M | T | W | T | F | S |
| | | | | 1 | 2 | 3 | 4 |
| 5 | 6 | 7 | 8 | 9 | 10 | 11 |
| 12 | 13 | 14 | 15 | 16 | 17 | 18 |
| 19 | 20 | 21 | 22 | 23 | 24 | 25 |
| 26 | 27 | 28 | 29 | 30 | | |

| DECEMBER | | | | | | |
|---|---|---|---|---|---|---|
| S | M | T | W | T | F | S |
| | | | | | 1 | 2 |
| 3 | 4 | 5 | 6 | 7 | 8 | 9 |
| 10 | 11 | 12 | 13 | 14 | 15 | 16 |
| 17 | 18 | 19 | 20 | 21 | 22 | 23 |
| 24 | 25 | 26 | 27 | 28 | 29 | 30 |

The suggested World Calendar with four equal quarters of 13 weeks. W is Worldsday, a world holiday which follows December 30 every year. L, another world holiday, is Leap Year Day and follows June 30 in leap years.

# Time in the Solar System

Scientific timekeeping is based on our knowledge of how the earth, the sun and distant stars move in relation to each other.

In the past the calendar and the clock have more or less corresponded to this motion to give us a rough basis for measuring time. But scientists today must have far more accurate knowledge of the motion of the heavens. Advances in physics, chemistry, biology and mathematics have made it necessary to measure time with great precision.

To achieve this precision, astronomers use the solar system and the universe as a giant timekeeper, while they improve and refine their observations. The measurement of time has become a science that serves all other sciences.

**How far does the earth rotate in one hour?**

When we look at the calendar to find out the date, we are, in a sense, checking a sky map that reveals the exact position of the earth in its orbit around the sun. And as the earth rotates on its axis, we know that the hour hand of the clock will move twice as fast. For every 15° of rotation the clock advances one hour. After the earth has rotated 360°, the hour hand has turned two full circles and the day is completed.

The interval of time necessary for the earth to travel around the sun is defined as a year or, more scientifically, as a *solar year*. It is 365 days, 5 hours, 48

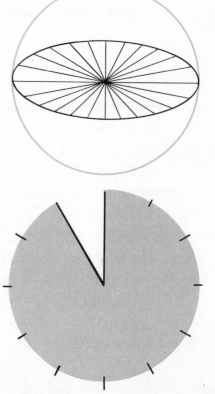

While the earth makes one full turn on its axis, the hour hand of the clock has to turn twice around the dial; for every 15° of rotation the clock advances one hour.

minutes and 46 seconds long. Because the earth is in continuous motion, we find it convenient to measure the start and finish of a single solar year from one vernal equinox to the next vernal equinox (see Figure 3 on page 24).

As the earth continues in its orbit, it creates one of the **When do the sun's rays slant the most? the least?** great cycles of nature in which the four seasons follow each other in a sequence that is repeated every year. If the earth stood still instead of pursuing its path around the sun, the climate in any specific location would always be the same. The climate and the seasons vary because the constant motion of the earth changes the angle of sunlight. A description of how the angle of sunlight affects the seasons is given in Figure 6 on page 25.

On other planets, the seasons and units **Where does a year equal a day?** of time vary greatly from those we know on earth. An inhabitant of the ringed planet Saturn would live with a day that is 10 hours and 12 minutes of our time and a year that equals 29½ of our years. Through the telescope we observe that the planet Venus takes 7½ months to journey around the sun, while the planet Mars makes the trip in 687 days and has seasons about double the length of the earth's.

A Neptunian year equals 165 earth years, but a day on this distant planet lasts only 15 hours and 45 minutes when timed by our clock. A calendar printed for Mercury would show no difference between a year and a day, because the period of rotation is identical to the period required to complete a full orbit.

Our sun is one of many stars in the universe. There is some evidence that, like our sun, other stars have planets revolving around them. The calculation of time on one of these planets would not be in any way related to the movements of our solar system. For an inhabitant of that planet, time would depend solely on the star (sun) of the solar system in which he lived.

If we look beyond our own solar system **What is a light year?** into other areas of the universe, the distances become so great that we cannot use ordinary systems of measurement. We have to describe these distances in *light years*, a special unit of measurement that combines both distance and time.

A light year is the distance that light travels in one year. The velocity of light is 186,000 miles per second, and one light year is approximately six trillion miles.

One light year = 186,000
× 60 (number of seconds in a minute)
× 60 (number of minutes in an hour)
× 24 (number of hours in a day)
× 365¼ (number of days in a year)
    = 5,880,000,000,000 miles
or approximately six trillion miles.

When we say that Alpha Centauri, the nearest star, is 4⅓ light years away, we mean that its distance from the earth is 4⅓ × 6 trillion, or 26 trillion miles.

But a light year gives us information about time as well as distance, and we can also state that light from the star will take 4⅓ years to reach the earth.

Light from our own star, the sun, takes only a little more than 8 minutes to reach us. The Andromeda Galaxy, which can be seen on a clear night without a telescope, is 2 million light years away — a distance of 9 billion billion miles.

Like all planets in our solar system, the

**Can we rely on the sun to measure time?**

earth revolves in its orbit and rotates on its axis at the same time. During rotation, the sun crosses each meridian (Figure 2 on page 24) every 24 hours. The time that elapses from one noon to the next, that is, the time between two successive crossings of the same meridian is called an *apparent solar day*. A sun dial that is carefully designed will therefore measure the hours and minutes in apparent solar time.

The sun, however, is an unreliable guide for accurate timekeeping. The velocity of the earth in its orbit varies throughout the year, causing the apparent motion of the sun to appear irregular. The word "apparent" is used because what seems to be the movement of the sun is actually the movement of the earth.

Apparent solar days reflect the irregularity of the earth's velocity and are not equal in length. Days measured by apparent solar time in July average 15 seconds shorter than the days in January, and December 25 is 50 seconds longer than September 13.

To produce days of identical length, it

**Why do we use an imaginary sun for timekeeping?**

was necessary to compromise with the solar system. Scientists created an imaginary or hypothetical sun which moves through space with a mean, or average, velocity of all the actual velocities that the real sun has. They also ignored the variations in velocity of the earth as it rotates on its axis and follows its orbit around the sun. In this *mean solar system* the length of the year is not changed, but the days are all assigned an equal length of 24 hours each. Mean solar time is frequently called *local time*.

The imaginary sun of the mean solar

**What is a standard time zone?**

system travels from the east to the west and circles the globe in exactly 24 hours. Longitudes 1° to the east of us are 4 minutes ahead in local time, and those 1° to the west, where the sun has not yet arrived, are 4 minutes behind.

Today, each band of longitude (see Figure 2 on page 24) has its own local time. Years ago, when clocks varied from town to town, it was difficult for travelers to meet train schedules and to make appointments even short distances away. In 1883, the United States and Canadian railroads adopted a system for standard time.

In 1918, the United States Congress passed a law establishing the four Standard Time Zones that we use today in the United States.

A meridian of 15° of longitude separates each zone. The dividing lines,

CONTINUED ON PAGE 26

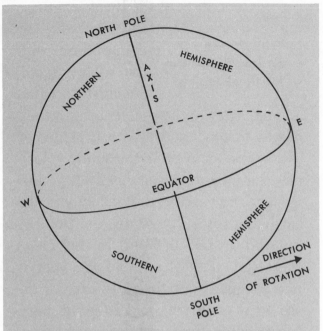

## Figure 1. HEMISPHERES OF THE EARTH

The equator is halfway between the two poles and divides the earth into the Northern and Southern Hemispheres. The earth rotates on its axis at a velocity of approximately 1000 miles per hour at the equator. It takes the earth 24 hours to turn completely through one full rotation.

## Figure 2. GREAT CIRCLES OF LONGITUDE

The meridians of longitude are imaginary circles of equal size which pass through both poles. Greenwich, England, is on the zero meridian. To the east, meridians are numbered 15° E, 30° E, 45° E, etc. Those to the west are numbered 15° W, 30° W, 45° W until 180° W, which is the same longitude as 180° E. The earth rotates 15° or the distance from one meridian to the next in 1 hour.

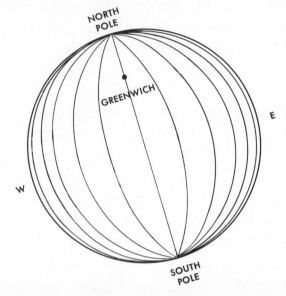

## Figure 4. LONG DAYS AND SHORT NIGHTS

On June 21 there are 24 hours of daylight in the North Pole region and 24 hours of darkness at the South Pole. During the summer, countries in the northernmost parts of the Northern Hemisphere have the longest days and shortest nights. In Stockholm, some summer days last for 19 hours while the nights are only 5 hours long.

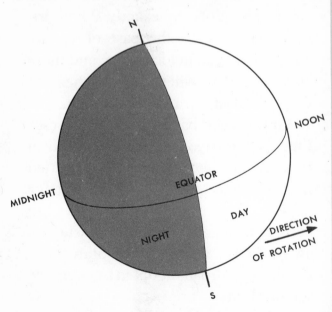

## Figure 3. WHEN DAY EQUALS NIGHT

On or about the dates March 21 and September 23, the sun is directly above the equator, and night and day are each 12 hours long everywhere in the world. March 21 is called the vernal equinox and September 23, the autumnal equinox.

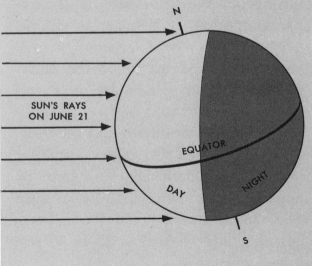

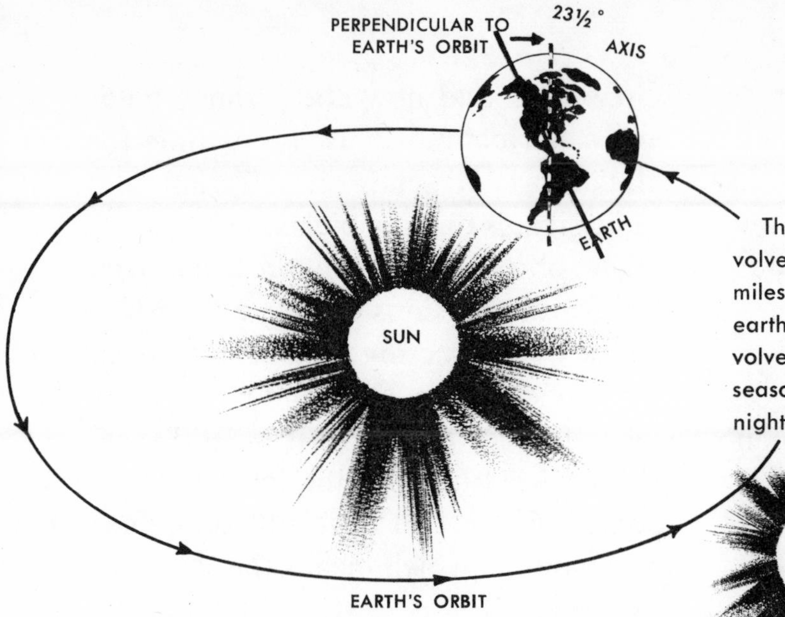

PERPENDICULAR TO
EARTH'S ORBIT
23½°
AXIS

SUN

EARTH

EARTH'S ORBIT

## Figure 5.  ORBIT OF THE EARTH

The earth follows the path of an ellipse as it revolves around the sun. Moving at a velocity of 18.5
miles per second (666,000 miles per hour), the
earth takes one year to make a full trip. As it revolves through its orbit around the sun (causing the
seasons), the earth also rotates on its axis (causing
night and day).

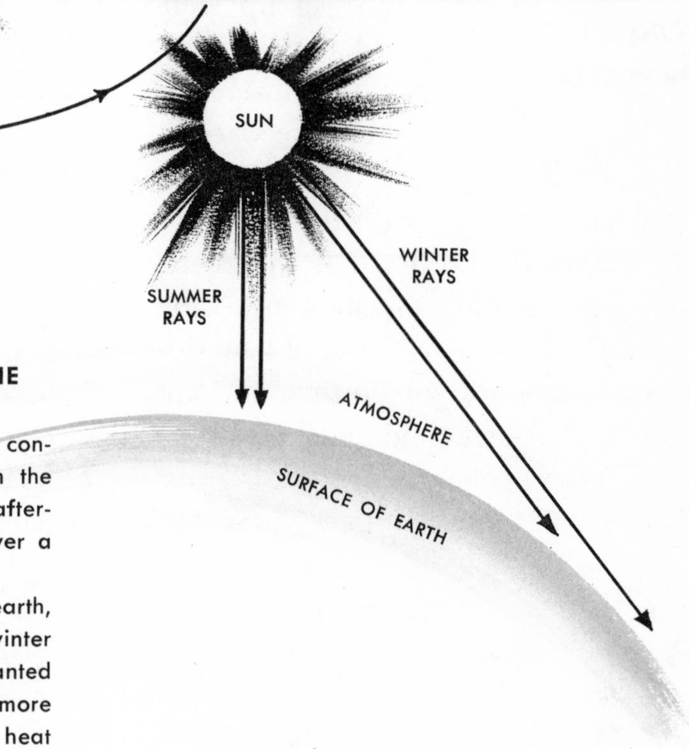

SUN

WINTER
RAYS

SUMMER
RAYS

ATMOSPHERE

SURFACE OF EARTH

## Figure 6.  SEASONAL VARIATION OF THE ANGLE OF SUNLIGHT

The vertical beams of summer sunlight are con-
centrated and produce maximum heat. When the
beams slant, as in the winter (or morning and after-
noon of any season), they are thinned out over a
greater area and the heat is less intense.

Before the beams reach the surface of the earth,
they lose some heat to the atmosphere. In the winter
the volume of atmosphere through which the slanted
beams pass is larger than in summer and thus more
heat is absorbed. During the winter this loss of heat
to the atmosphere causes the surface of the earth to
be colder than it is in the summer.

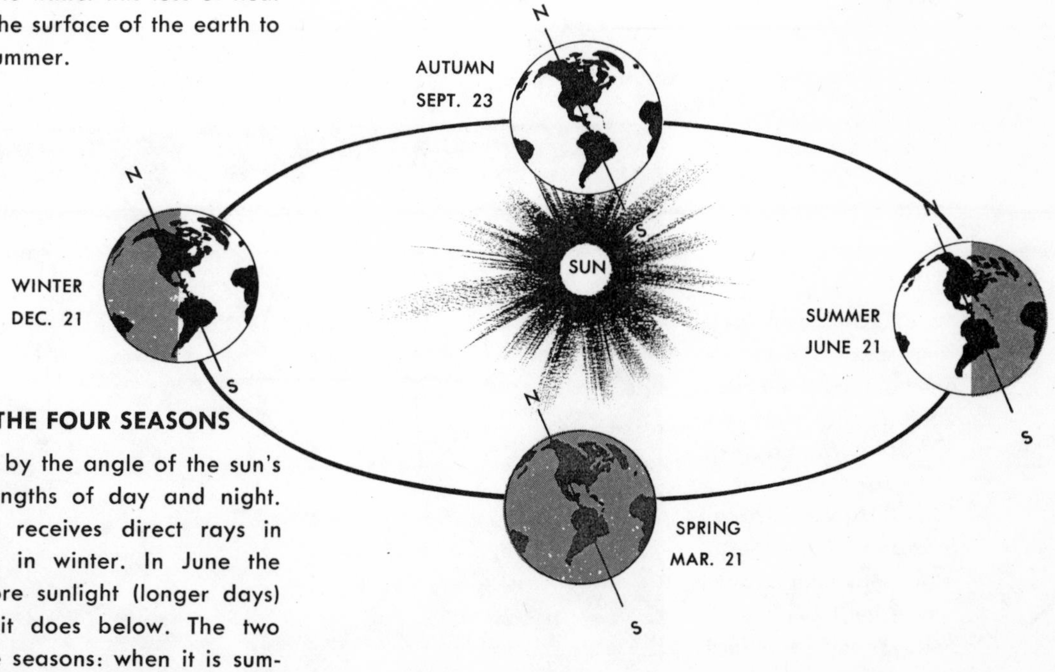

AUTUMN
SEPT. 23

N

WINTER
DEC. 21

N

S

SUN

N

S

SUMMER
JUNE 21

S

N

S

SPRING
MAR. 21

S

## Figure 7.  ORBIT OF THE FOUR SEASONS

The seasons are caused by the angle of the sun's
rays and the changing lengths of day and night.
The Northern Hemisphere receives direct rays in
summer and slanted rays in winter. In June the
rotating earth receives more sunlight (longer days)
above the equator than it does below. The two
hemispheres have opposite seasons: when it is summer in New York, it is winter in Sydney, Australia.

however, are not straight in order to accommodate some state borders and railroad terminals. The 15° interval was chosen because it takes one hour for the sun to complete its apparent journey through this distance.

One year after the United States Congress set up standard time zones, an international body agreed on a corresponding system for countries everywhere. Starting with 0° at Greenwich, England, the 360° of the globe were split up into 24 standard time meridians of 15° each. The 24 meridians are one hour apart in time and are the basis for exact time determinations on the entire globe.

The Royal Observatory, formerly at Greenwich and now about thirty miles away at Herstmonceux, keeps time for all nations and sends out telegraph and radio signals that are picked up by ships, other observatories and astronomers. Navigators on ships calculate their longitude by subtracting the local time from Greenwich Mean Time and multiplying the difference by 15°. If it is 3:00 P.M. Greenwich time and the local time on board ship is 1:00 P.M., the difference is two hours, which means the ship is in longitude 30° west.

**Where is the time center for the whole world?**

U.S. Eastern Standard Time is 5 hours behind Greenwich Time

U.S. Central Standard Time is 6 hours behind Greenwich Time

U.S. Mountain Standard Time is 7 hours behind Greenwich Time

U.S. Pacific Standard Time is 8 hours behind Greenwich Time

PACIFIC TIME    MOUNTAIN TIME    CENTRAL TIME    EASTERN TIME.

American Standard Time zones: The time is one hour earlier in each zone to the west. At 11:00 A.M. Eastern Standard Time, it is 10:00 A.M. Central Standard Time, 9:00 A.M. Mountain Standard Time, and 8:00 A.M. Pacific Standard Time.

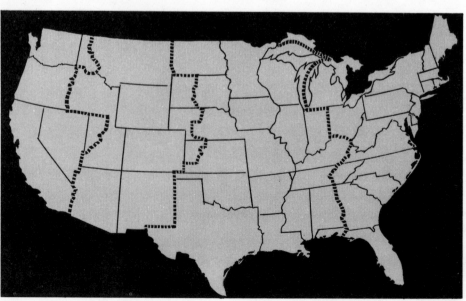

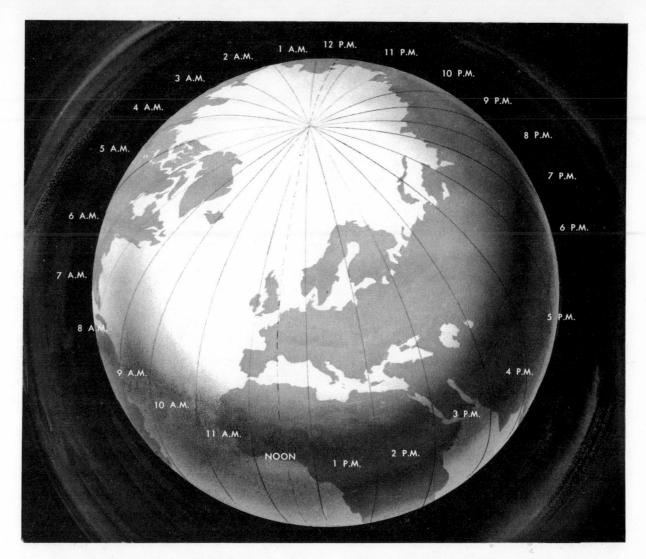

The international Standard Time Zones are based on the 0° zone at Greenwich being equal to noon.

## STANDARD TIMES IN DIFFERENT CITIES OF THE WORLD

In some countries the standard time differs from the assigned meridian time because of special local or national requirements. The standard time in several foreign cities is compared below with that of New York City at 12:00 noon Eastern Standard Time.

| | | | |
|---|---|---|---|
| Amsterdam | 6:00 P.M. | Hong Kong | 1:00 A.M. |
| Bangkok | 12:00 Mid. | | (next morning) |
| Bogota | 12:00 Noon | London | 5:00 P.M. |
| | (same time) | Moscow | 8:00 P.M. |
| Buenos Aires | 2:00 P.M. | Paris | 6:00 P.M. |
| Delhi | 10:30 P.M. | Mexico City | 11:00 A.M. |
| Havana | 12:00 Noon | Tokyo | 2:00 A.M. |
| | (same time) | | (next morning) |

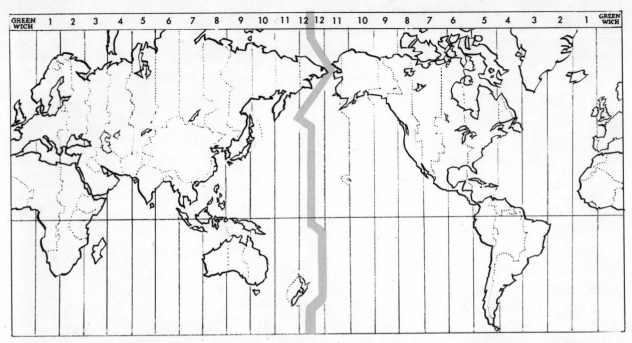

The imaginary line at the 180th meridian is the International Date Line. Notice how the Date Line curves away from the 180th meridian to avoid cutting through the eastern tip of Asia and some of the Island groups.

Halfway around the globe from Greenwich, at the 180° meridian of longitude, is the International Date Line, where the day begins. Here, today may become tomorrow or it may change into yesterday, depending on your direction of travel.

**How can you lose or gain a day?**

Each side of the Date Line has a different day. To the west it is a day later; to the east a day earlier. When you start out from the west on a Sunday and cross the Date Line, the day becomes yesterday, or Saturday. Reversing your route and traveling on a Saturday from east to west, the day becomes tomorrow, or Sunday. The whole world has the same day only on the instant that midnight occurs on the Date Line.

The calculations of astronomers frequently require the use of *sidereal time* (from *sidus*, the Latin word for star). Sidereal time, or star time, corrects a

**What is star time?**

flaw in our measurement of the earth's rotation, so that a more accurate study of the heavens is possible.

After the earth has completed a full rotation of 360°, it must turn approximately 1° more to resume the same relative position it had to the sun 24 hours earlier. The small additional turn enables the earth to compensate for the distance it travels in orbit while it rotates. A more accurate measurement of the 360° rotation is possible if the earth is checked against a bright star whose great distance makes the amount of earth's orbital travel of little mathematical importance. The sidereal day produced by this measurement is the time that the earth requires to complete one rotation with respect to the stars.

The day calculated by the stars is about 4 minutes shorter than the mean solar day and cannot be used for regulating civil affairs. If

**Why is star time unpractical?**

we tried to keep time by the sidereal system, which is always ahead of the sun's cycle, the sidereal clock would lose 4 minutes from every solar day. Because the lost minutes would add up from day to day, the clocks and watches that we use, which are guided by the position of the sun, would become practically useless.

On about March 21, when the noon sun is directly overhead, both the sidereal and solar systems have the same time. One month later, a person who lived by the sidereal system would find that at noon solar time his clock read two P.M. Three months after March 21, instead of indicating noon, his clock would tell him that it was six P.M.

Regular events, like meals, working hours, and sleep would follow a confusing schedule that changed daily.

Astronomers work with the sidereal system, but the clocks and watches that we use for ordinary purposes are regulated to mean solar time.

We divide the day into two 12-hour periods, and although the hours are calculated from the position of the noon sun, the day itself officially starts at midnight. The first 12 hours are designated A.M. (from the Latin *ante meridiem,* meaning before noon), and the 12 hours that follow noon are designated P. M. (from the Latin *post meridiem,* meaning after noon).

**What time system is used by the armed services?**

The United States military forces and some European countries avoid the possibilities of error and confusion in the A.M. and P.M. system by using a 24-hour clock. Here are some examples of the 24-hour clock:

| A.M. AND P.M. CLOCK | 24-HOUR CLOCK |
|---|---|
| 9:00 A.M. | 0900 |
| 2:15 A.M. | 0215 |
| 12:00 noon | 1200 |
| 12:00 midnight | 0000 |
| 3:30 P.M. | 1530 |
| 11:59 P.M. | 2359 |

**How are the hours of daylight increased?**

Another change in the time system, known as Daylight Saving Time, created extremes of antagonism and popular approval when it was first discussed by the public.

The London builder, William Willett, who proposed Daylight Saving Time in 1907, wanted to give people more opportunity to enjoy the outdoors after they finished work. He suggested that the best way to gain such leisure

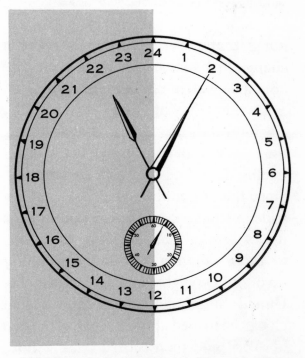

A 24-hour clock eliminates possible confusion.

was to advance the clock one hour during the time of long summer daylight.

Willett was promptly called a humanitarian by his admirers. With equal promptness, he was called a lunatic by many detractors, some of whom accused him of meddling with "God's time." Of course there is no timekeeping system, either scientific or religious, that can be called God's time. Ever since astronomy became a science, the

Farmers frequently oppose Daylight Savings Time. They claim, with understandable indignation, that they and their livestock get up early enough even when the clock is set at Standard Time.

hours that govern the day have been changed by forward thinking men who hoped to better our way of living.

Daylight Saving Time was tried by England and the United States during the first World War as a control for reducing fuel and power consumption. Since then its adoption has been nationwide in England, but in our country the use of Daylight Saving Time is limited to those communities and states that favor it. Daylight Saving Time in the United States generally requires that clocks be turned ahead 1 hour at the end of April and then turned back 1 hour at the end of September or October.

Follow the path of a star for 2 consecutive nights, and you will discover how astronomers use the universe to check time. On the second night you will see the star appear at the identical spot in the heavens 3 minutes and 56 seconds earlier than it did on the first night. Thus if a star is in a certain position at 9:15 P.M., the next night it will be in the same position at 4 seconds after 9:11 P.M. You can use this dependable time relationship between the earth and the stars to find out how accurately your watch keeps time.

Stand at a window that faces south and select a chimney or the edge of a high building to be your reference guide. Then tape a piece of cardboard which has a small hole in it to the window. The cardboard should be positioned so that you can see the reference guide and also observe some of the nearby stars.

Do not confuse a star with a planet. Because of their great distance from the earth, stars generally appear smaller than planets. They have a twinkling light, while planets reflect a steady, more constant light. Another and perhaps better way to tell whether a body in the heavens is a star or a planet, is to study its movement for a few nights. A planet moves independently into new positions when observed against the background of the other heavenly bodies; stars appear to move in groups or constellations.

After you have viewed the movements of some of the stars towards your building or chimney reference guide, choose one of them for your time experiment. As soon as this star disappears behind the reference guide, write down the exact time shown on your watch.

The next night, with the cardboard still in position, use the same star and the same reference guide and repeat your observation.

If your watch is accurate, the star will disappear 3 minutes and 56 seconds sooner than the previous night. A watch that is slow will show a greater time loss. One that is fast will show less of a time loss.

Lining up a star to check your watch.

## HOW TO FIND DIRECTIONS BY USING YOUR WATCH AND THE SUN

You can turn your watch into a compass any day that the sun is shining. First create a shadow pole by setting a small twig or a matchstick into the ground so that it stands straight up. Then place your watch flat on the ground with its edge against the shadow pole. Turn the watch until the hour hand is covered by the shadow. The hour hand is now pointing directly at the sun.

South lies halfway between the hour hand and the number 12. As an example, imagine that the shadow falls on 4. The number 2 would then point south. If you then face south, west is to your right, east to your left, and north behind you. If you are in an area using daylight saving time, it is easy to make a correction for the hour that your watch is set ahead. Follow the same procedure with only one change: find south by taking the halfway mark between the hour hand and the number 1.

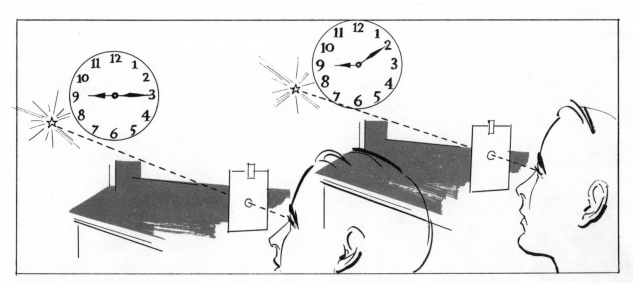

# Timekeepers From Fire to the Atom

Scientists have learned to split time into fragments smaller than a billionth of a second. By inducing vibrations in selected atoms, they developed an atomic clock that represents the greatest advance ever made in the fine division of time. The long growth that ultimately led from the first timekeepers to an understanding of the energy of a vibrating atom, reflects great changes in the social and scientific background of time measurement. Our present-day atomic clock is the product of many profound advances in science. Its distant ancestors were created from far simpler resources, like fire, water, sand and sun.

**How did fire help to tell time?**

Some of the first attempts to record time utilized the slow and regular burning of a fuel. Back in a remote period of Chinese history, dampened ropes were knotted at equal intervals and then ignited. As the fire smoldered past each knot, approximate units of time were counted off.

A similar timekeeper made of candles was invented in 870 A.D. by Alfred the Great of England. Each candle lasted four hours and had three markings per hour. After one candle burned down, Alfred's priests lit another, maintaining a perpetual candle clock that consumed itself. Oil lamps were also used to subdivide the day. The reservoir had a vertical scale which measured the decreasing level of the oil as it burned through the wick.

**Where does the rod of a sundial point?**

We do not know the exact date when sundials were first used, but they are at least 4,000 years old and are of Babylonian origin. About 700 B.C., the Biblical prophet Isaiah comforted the sick king Hezekiah by causing time to move backward on the sundial of Ahaz. The story is told in the thirty-eighth chapter of Isaiah:

"Behold, I will bring again the shadow of the degrees, which has gone down in the sundial of Ahaz, ten degrees backward. So the sun returned ten degrees, by which degrees it was gone down."

All sundials measure apparent solar time. They generally have a rod that casts a shadow on a dial made with lines for the different hours.

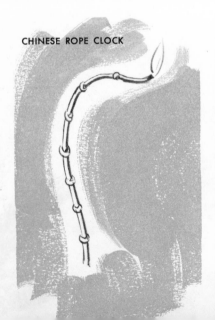

CHINESE ROPE CLOCK

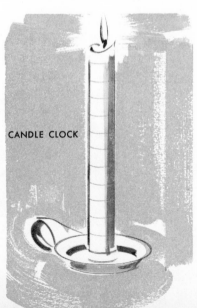

CANDLE CLOCK

OIL CLOCK

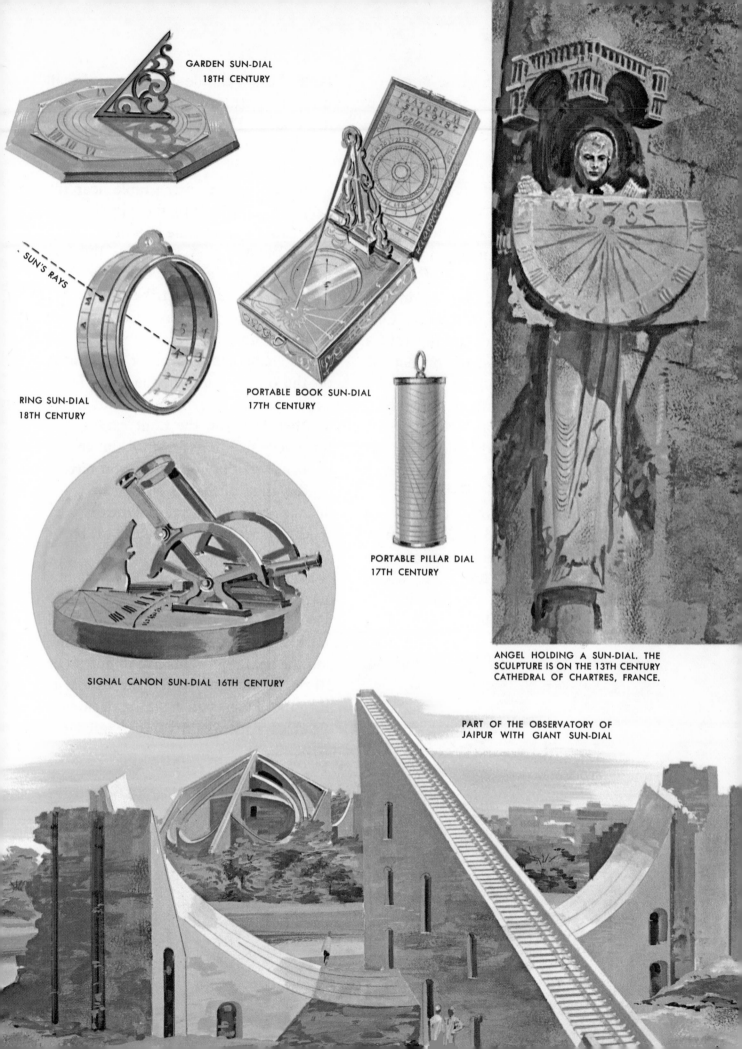

GARDEN SUN-DIAL
18TH CENTURY

SUN'S RAYS

RING SUN-DIAL
18TH CENTURY

PORTABLE BOOK SUN-DIAL
17TH CENTURY

PORTABLE PILLAR DIAL
17TH CENTURY

SIGNAL CANON SUN-DIAL 16TH CENTURY

ANGEL HOLDING A SUN-DIAL. THE
SCULPTURE IS ON THE 13TH CENTURY
CATHEDRAL OF CHARTRES, FRANCE.

PART OF THE OBSERVATORY OF
JAIPUR WITH GIANT SUN-DIAL

The rod points to the true north or south pole, and is built to form an angle with the dial equal to the latitude where the sundial is located.

Some sundials were crude and inaccurate while others produced surprisingly precise measurements. Their sizes and shapes varied from the small pocket instruments, popular in the eighteenth century, to the giant sundial of Jaipur, India, which has a dial 100 feet in diameter and a rod 147 feet long. One unusual European sundial of the 1500's used a magnifying glass to concentrate the rays of the noon sun on the powder charge of a small cannon. The blast, like a 12 o'clock factory whistle, was a time signal to everybody who heard it.

### HOW TO MAKE A CANDLE CLOCK

Obtain two candles, about five inches long. Through a small piece of board, about half an inch thick, hammer two nails about an inch long, and about an inch apart. Place the board, with the nail points sticking up, on a table. Push a candle down on each nail until the bottom of the candle touches the board. The candles are now held steady so that they will not fall over when lit.

Place a watch on the table near the candles. Light one of the candles, and note exactly what time you lit it. (CAUTION! Be sure that you close the box of matches or the cover of the book of matches before you strike a match!)

When the candle has burned for five minutes, note how far down it has burned, and make a mark or scratch on the other candle at the same level. Wait another five minutes, and make another mark on the unlit candle. Do this every five minutes until the candle is burned to the bottom. If you have a candle that burns so slowly that the distance burned in five minutes is very small, mark the unlit candle at 10 or 15 minute intervals.

With water-colors or other paints, mark circles around the unlit candle where you have made time-interval marks. The distance between one ring and the next represents five minutes (or 10 or 15 minutes) when the candle is burning. Thus, you have made a candle clock with which you can tell time.

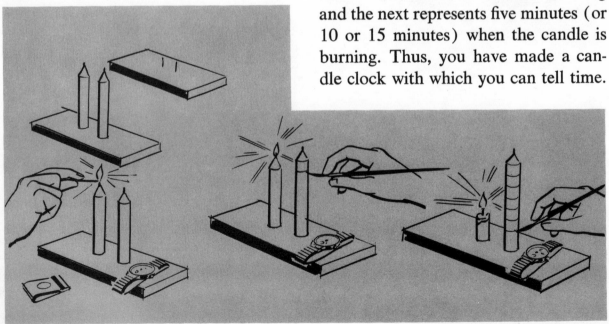

## HOW TO MAKE A SUNDIAL

Obtain a flat board, about one foot square. Using a drawing compass or a pencil on the end of a string, draw a circle eight inches in diameter on the board. In the center of the circle, glue or cement a wooden spool of the kind on which thread is wound. Make sure that the hole in the center of the spool is directly over the center of the circle. Place a sharpened pencil, eraser end down, into the hole in the spool. You may have to shave the end of the pencil with a knife or sandpaper, and remove the eraser, in order to make the pencil fit into the hole.

Hammer a nail a short distance into the board, near one corner. Make sure the nail is long enough so that it sticks up higher than the top of the spool. Just before dawn on a sunny day, place the board on a window sill that faces south on flat, open ground, or on some other horizontal support where sunlight can reach it all day long. With your eye on a level with the top of the spool, pick out some object several feet away, perhaps the edge of a window in a house down the street. Then turn the board so that you see the pencil, the nail, and the distant object in a straight line. Leave the board in this position.

As soon as the sun begins to cast the shadow of the pencil on the board, note the time on your watch or listen for radio time signals. When the first hour on the hour arrives — for example, 7 a.m. — make a pencil mark on the board exactly where the shadow of the pencil point is. Label this mark 7. Do the same at eight o'clock and each hour thereafter until sundown, labeling each mark with the number of the hour at which the mark was made. For instance, at four p.m., make a mark at the point of the pencil and number it 4. At the last hour on the hour before sundown, you will have completed your sundial.

Whenever you want to use the sundial, you must place it *in exactly the same position* as it was when you made it. To do this, sight along the pencil, the nail, and the distant object, just as you did when first putting the board into position. To tell time by the sundial, note where the shadow of the pencil point is. Suppose it is halfway between the 10 and 11 marks on the board; then the time is 10:30. If the shadow is three-quarters of the distance between the 2 and 3 marks, then the time is 2:45.

The only "clock" Columbus had on his ship was a half-hour sandglass.

In the Greek clepsydra (above), the water dropped out of the vessel. In the Chinese version (below), the vessel filled itself with water. In both cases, the markings for the time were inside the vessels.

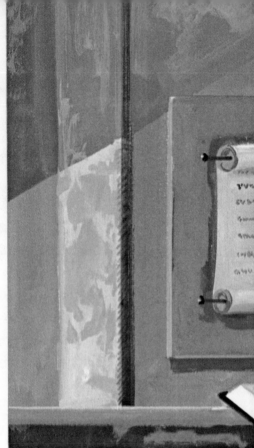

Some monasteries in the Middle Ages used a "psalm clock" to count the hours of their devotions and duties. Every psalm was chanted at the same speed, and the number of a specific psalm told the hour. As soon as one monk was tired, another took his place and continued to chant.

In about two weeks your sundial will no longer tell time accurately. Each week for six months from the time you made your sundial, it will become less and less accurate.

Why does the accuracy of your sundial change? Because as the earth orbits around the sun, the sun's path across the sky changes. It moves south for six months and north for the other six. Does this mean that we cannot make a sundial that is accurate all year around? No, but it took astronomers many centuries to learn how to make an accurate sundial, and the mathematics that they used are somewhat complicated.

You will find that as you approach a period that is one year after you made your sundial, it will become more and more accurate. On the exact anniversary date, your sundial will tell the correct time again.

Sundials are useless at night or on cloudy days. Two other early timekeepers, the sandglass and the water clock, were used to compensate for this inadequacy.

**How were moving sand and moving water used to measure time?**

When the whole sandglass device is turned over, the sand streams through the channel at a fairly uniform speed.

36

into an elaborate and ingenious mechanism that performed many operations, like indicating the hour by ringing bells, beating drums, blowing trumpets or the movement of tiny figures.

The introduction of devices such as gears, racks and dials into the clepsydra greatly expanded and refined the science

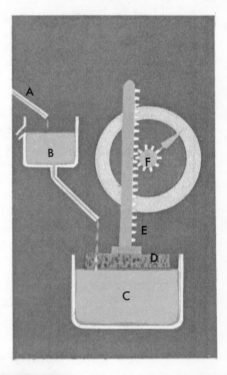

Water is supplied continuously from a pipe into reservoir B, from where it slowly drips into tank C. An overflow tube keeps the level in the reservoir constant. As the level of water in tank C rises, rack E is pushed up by float D. The rack turns geared wheel F, and the hand of the clock moves the dial to indicate the hour.

The length of time it takes for the sand to empty from the top globe into the bottom one is determined by the size of the globes, the amount of sand and the diameter of the channel.

Like the sandglass, the water clock, known as the *clepsydra* (meaning "water thief" in Greek), did not depend on sunlight to tell time. The earliest type of water clock used by the Greeks and Romans was a large bowl with markings on the inside and a hole in the bottom. As the water escaped through the hole, the different markings would be exposed and indicate the passing of hours. In China and India a small brass bowl that was pierced in the bottom was floated on a basin of water. The floating bowl would gradually fill with water, and after a measured interval of time, it would sink. An attendant then struck a gong and set the bowl afloat again.

The clepsydra eventually developed

This clepsydra from the 18th century is based on the principles of the waterclock of Ctesibius of Alexandria about 140 B.C. As water runs out of the container, it turns a set of waterwheels which cause the figure with the pointer to rise and indicate the hours on the column. The mechanism in the lower part of the column which our illustration shows exposed, is actually covered and beautifully camouflaged.

37

of measuring time. What followed was an improvement in timekeepers that would not have been possible without these devices: the substitution of mechanical power for water power.

### MAKE YOUR OWN WATERCLOCK:

Take an empty milk container and punch a little hole in it near the bottom. Fill the container with colored water and place it in a basin. The water will drip out slowly. By holding the container to the light or holding a flashlight against it, you will be able to see the water level inside the container. Mark the level on the outside after every 15 minutes. You have made a waterclock. It is a primitive one, but it will work.

### HOW TO MAKE A SAND GLASS

Obtain two identical glass jars with screw caps. Remove the caps and glue or cement them top-to-top, as in the illustration. Using a block of wood, as shown, and a very thin nail called a brad, make a hole through both jar caps.

Obtain enough sand to almost fill one of the jars. The sand must be dry and clean. To be sure that the sand is clean, sieve it through some wire mesh, like that used to make window screens. It will be even better if, after sieving the sand through wire mesh, you further sieve it through muslin or some other coarse mesh cloth.

Put the clean, dry sand into one bottle. Screw the caps onto this bottle.

Then, screw the other bottle into the other cap. Turn the bottle around so that the empty bottle is on the bottom. Note on a watch with a second hand the exact time you turned the bottles. Then, note the time when the last of the sand falls from the upper to the lower bottle. By doing this, you will find out how long it took the sand to run from one bottle into the other.

Let us suppose that it took 7½ minutes for the sand to run from the upper to the lower bottle. (The time may be quite different, depending on the size of the bottles you use.) Now 7½ minutes is an odd time that is not of much use in a timer. So you will want to regulate your sand glass to time a more useful interval, such as five minutes. To do this, pour out a little sand from the bottle, but don't throw it away. Put the bottles together, and again time how long it takes sand to run from one to another. If the time is still more than five minutes, pour out more sand; if the time is less than five minutes, add a little sand. Continue adding and subtracting sand, until it takes exactly five

minutes for the sand to run from one bottle into the other. Now you have a sand glass that will time exactly five minutes.

The first mechanical clocks were bulky

**How did the first mechanical clocks look?**

giants that weighed several tons and frequently were forged in a blacksmith's shop. They did not have dials but used jointed figures of people, known as "Jacks," to strike the hour or quarter hour.

Falling weights were employed to drive these clocks. The weight was attached to a rope that was wound around a drum. As the weight fell, the rope would uncoil and turn the drum. A single revolving clock hand or bell striker fastened to the end of the drum indicated or signaled the hour.

One clock belonging to this period, is generally recognized as the direct ancestor of modern mechanical timekeepers. It was built by the German Henry De Vick in 1360 for Charles V of France and it is still standing in Paris with one hour hand pointing to the time on the dial.

All clocks and watches, from the early

**What are the four parts used in all clocks and watches?**

ones like De Vick's to those that are produced today, have four basic parts:

The *driving mechanism* is the source of energy and keeps the clock or watch running. It may be a weight, a coiled spring, or an electric motor.

The first mechanical timepieces had no dial and no hands, only tolling bells or Jacks to strike the hour.

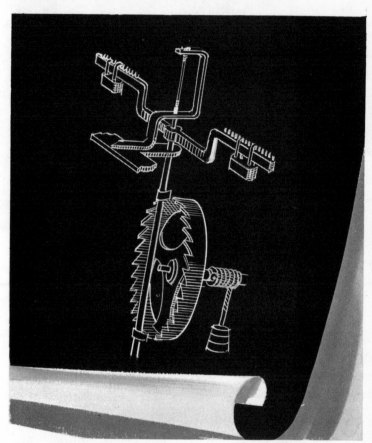

The primitive escapement (transmission) with its foliot (a kind of balance that worked as controlling mechanism) and the weight on a turning drum (driving mechanism). That was all the mechanism the first clocks had.

The driving mechanism in an electric clock is an electric motor whose speed is controlled by the 60 cycle per second

39

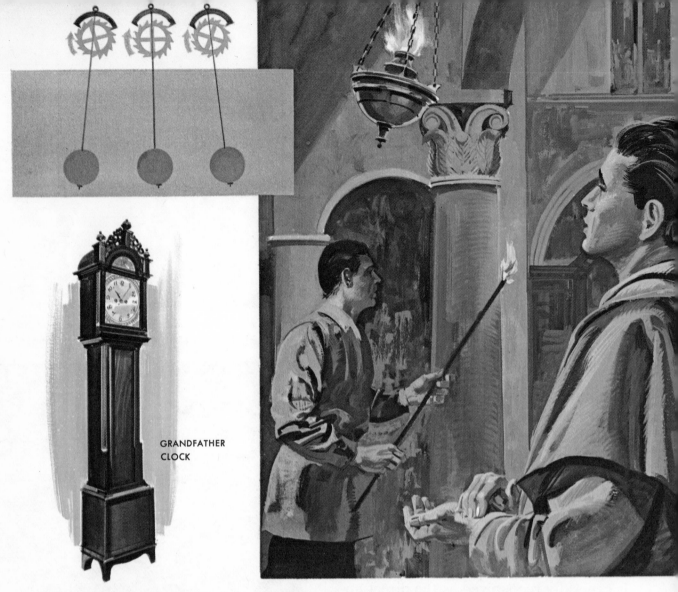

GRANDFATHER
CLOCK

At the end of the 16th century the Italian astronomer, physicist and mathematician, Galileo, noticed that the chandelier which illuminated the altar of the cathedral of Pisa swayed with the slightest stir of wind. He observed that, no matter how far the chandelier swung, it always took the same time to swing back. He checked his observation by timing the swings with his own pulse. Galileo himself applied this discovery to the mechanical clock. It meant that by attaching a pendulum to the pallet, it could be made to stop and release the geared wheel at the same rate regardless of the amount of force applied.

A.C. current that enters most homes. The motor revolves 3600 times per minute and is geared down to the required speeds for the clock hands.

The *transmission* distributes the energy through a train of connected gears that turn the clock hands.

The *controlling mechanism*, perhaps the most important part of any timepiece, brakes the energy so that it is released slowly. The hour hand is permitted to rotate once in 12 hours, the minute hand once in 60 minutes, and the second hand once in 60 seconds.

A *dial* for reading the time is necessary to complete the clock.

After De Vick's work, the inventions

**How were clocks reduced in size?**

that most revolutionized the construction of clocks were the mainspring and the pendulum.

In 1500 Peter Henlein, a German locksmith, substituted a ribbon of

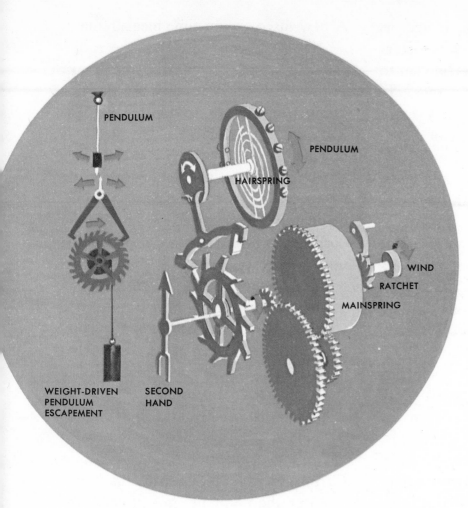

PENDULUM

PENDULUM

HAIRSPRING

WIND

RATCHET

MAINSPRING

WEIGHT-DRIVEN
PENDULUM
ESCAPEMENT

SECOND
HAND

Modern wristwatch, the Hamilton Electric, in which the power source is a tiny battery the size of a button.

The pendulum usually is a rod pivoted at one end and weighted at the other. The longer the rod or the lighter the weight, the slower the swings. With this knowledge it became possible to adjust the pendulum to swing exactly once in a second. If the pendulum would be attached just to a ratchet that would drive the clock hands, the pendulum would gradually cease to swing on account of the friction. Some form of stored energy had to be used to keep the gear train in motion. Hanging weights with cords coiled around a rotable drum provided this energy at first. Later a coiled spring was used for energy supply. In wrist watches, the hanging pendulum of the grandfather clock is replaced by a hairspring driven flat balance wheel.

spring steel for the weight that had always been used to drive clocks. The elimination of the heavy weight made portable timepieces possible. By the 1600's, small pocket watches using mainsprings were in style.

One hundred and fifty-eight years after the introduction of the mainspring, the great Dutch scientist Christian Huygens

**Why are pendulum clocks so accurate?**

built a clock that used a pendulum for the controlling mechanism. A pendulum is any free swinging object, such as a weight hanging from a string, which has a back and forth motion. The laws that describe the movement of pendulums had been worked out by Galileo in 1583.

The time of successive swings of a pendulum is fairly constant, and Huygens was able to regulate the clock to an excellent accuracy. As the pendulum travels back and forth, it acts as a very fine control that uniformly meters the energy of the driving mechanism to the clock hands. Smaller swings are always preferable because they more closely resemble the behavior of a perfect pendulum and minimize errors. Pendulum clocks are reliable and accurate for mechanical mechanisms, and are still being produced.

At one time elegance rather than accuracy was the criterion of a good timepiece. Many watches and clocks were works of great visual artistry, but often they would gain or lose as much as an hour daily. From the highly decorative ornament of the last few centuries, the timepiece of today has developed into an extraordinary machine that is still attractive but functions with precise efficiency.

**How many times does your watch tick in a day?**

The watch on your wrist performs mechanical wonders. One winding gives it the power to tick 5 times a second or 432,000 times a day. While the watch is ticking away, the rim of the large balance wheel travels about the equivalent of 7 miles and swings back and forth 540,000 times in a day. If the wheels of a car turned the same number of times, they would travel 250,000 miles in a year. The car would just about fall apart on a trip of that mileage but your watch, some of whose parts move an equivalent distance, might not need repairs for years.

A new discovery in time measurement, called the radiocarbon clock, uses the theories of nuclear physics to look back into history. The radiocarbon clock is powered by Carbon 14, which was manufactured by the action of cosmic rays passing through the earth's atmosphere thousands of years ago. When cosmic rays strike nitrogen atoms in the upper atmosphere (and this process goes on all the time), some of the nitrogen is transformed into radioactive Carbon 14. In turn, the Carbon 14 combines with the oxygen in the atmosphere to form carbon dioxide. Plants absorb the radioactive carbon dioxide along with their diet of normal carbon dioxide as long as they are alive. Animals develop a tissue structure that contains Carbon 14 when they eat the plants.

**What is a radiocarbon clock?**

After the plant or animal dies, the Carbon 14 continues to emit radioactive particles, whose strength can be measured with a Geiger counter. Over the years the intensity of the radiation decreases at a known rate. By comparing the intensity of the weakened radiation with that of fresh Carbon 14, the age of the plant or animal is determined. The plant or animal need not be preserved in its original form but can be checked for radiation even after it has been made into a tool or some other product of civilization.

Using the radiocarbon clock, physicists and archaeologists can look as far back as 28,000 years into the past. Their findings

**How old is ancient Jericho?**

tell part of the unrecorded story of ancient peoples. For example, the Biblical walled city of Jericho was found to be 9,000 years old. The remains of a charcoal fire reveal that people had inhabited the famous Lascaux Cave in France about 15,000 years ago. Since the application of the Carbon 14 test to archaeology, many of the former dating estimates could be confirmed or corrected.

Every modern device that tells time relies on the rhythmic beat or regular vibration of a controlling mechanism. In some clocks the control is achieved by the swing of a pendulum, while other clocks and wrist watches use a balance wheel coupled to a hair spring. An electric clock utilizes the steady frequency of 60 cycles per second generated by the power station. Frequency is the number of back and forth movements that anything, (for example, a wave of electric current) makes during 1 second.

**What type of motion is used in all clocks of today?**

Where critical precision is required, many laboratories use a quartz clock. Crystals like quartz have the ability to vibrate at a sharp, dependable rate when they are placed in an electronic circuit and stimulated by alternating currents of radio frequencies.

Once the quartz begins to vibrate at a uniform rate, it imposes its own natural frequency on the whole circuit. The modified current is then used to run an electric clock. The frequency of the current fed into the clock is so carefully regulated by the vibrating quartz, that

A marine chronometer is a highly accurate time-keeper used by ships at sea to find their longitude. It was never too difficult to find the latitude of the ship's position by observing the height of the sun, the moon or the stars. The exact longitude however can only be found if the sailor knew both the exact time at the port he had left and the local time at sea. While the local time at sea could be measured by the position of the sun, the time at the port had to come from a timepiece that would keep accurate time even after rough seas, storms and waves had rocked the captain's instruments. Such a foolproof clock is called a chronometer. About 1770, John Harrison, an Englishman, built the first successful marine chronometer and won the 20,000 pound prize described in a public proclamation of 1713: "The Lords Commissioners of the Admiralty hereby offer the sum of 20,000 pounds for any method whereby the Longitude can at all times be determined at sea; the whole reward to be given if the method, when tested by a voyage to the West Indies, is found to be within thirty miles of the truth, 15,000 pounds if within forty miles and 10,000 pounds if within sixty miles of the truth."

GERMAN IRON CLOCK
WITH FOLIOT (ABOUT 1400)

MODERN
MANTEL PIECE
CLOCK

LOUIS XV CLOCK (1750)

14TH CENTURY CLOCK IN
WELLS CATHEDRAL, ENGLAND

the loss or gain of time is sometimes as little as 1 second in 30 years.

For most laboratory problems, the quartz clock is a timekeeper of superb accuracy. Aging of the crystal and changes in the atmosphere, however, ultimately reduce its efficiency below the level needed to explore some highly advanced scientific areas. Among these are astronomical measurements of the earth's rotation, an improved system of navigation signals for airplanes, and the investigation of motion in atomic physics.

To find a clock for such work, one that would not be disturbed by aging or the atmosphere, scientists turned to the world of molecules and atoms. There they found the most dependable to-and-fro motion in all nature.

In 1949 the first atomic clock was built.

**How does an atomic clock work?** The ammonia molecule was used in this clock because its pyramid structure permits it to act as a pendulum, scaled down to atomic size. *Ammonia* is a gas that has three hydrogen atoms and one nitrogen atom. (The familiar *ammonia*, found on a grocer's shelf, is a cleaning solution made by dissolving ammonia gas in water.)

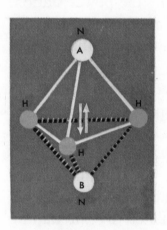

In the atomic clock, the nitrogen atom vibrates between points A and B at the incredible rate of 2,387 billion times per second. (N = nitrogen atom; H = hydrogen atom).

Examine the illustration and you will see that the hydrogen atoms occupy the lower corners of the pyramid, while the nitrogen atom is at the top. If extremely high frequency radio waves are used to excite the ammonia gas, the nitrogen atom will vibrate up and down between its normal top position A, and one an

44

LADY'S WATCH AND PIN
(LATE 19TH CENTURY)

PISTOL WATCH
(EARLY 19TH CENTURY)

MODERN WATCH IN
A LADY'S RING

At right, a German (Nuremberg) portable "table clock" of the 16th century. Above, side view of a modern pocket watch. Note the difference in thickness.

One of the most unique time-pieces in Europe is the Flower Clock at Interlaken, Switzerland. Year after year a new dial for this clock is provided by the planting of thousands of tiny plants and flowers. The mechanism of the clock is buried underground.

equal distance B, on the other side of the base.

The nitrogen atom can be thought of as a rapid-fire pendulum that sends out energy as it travels back and forth. This energy, like that of the quartz crystal, is piped off to an electric clock so that the time can be read directly. The ammonia clock does not vary in accuracy by more than 1 second in 15 years.

A clock that uses the gaseous form of the element *cesium* is one of the newest of the atomic timekeepers. The cesium clock is more accurate than the ammonia clock and can be built so that it does not lose or gain more than 1 second in 300 years.

From observatories where quartz or atomic clocks are used astronomers send out time signals every hour. These signals are relayed by radio and telephone to aircraft, ships and installations all over the world. Our communication satellite, the Telstar, will be used to transmit time signals at the fastest and most accurate rate yet known.

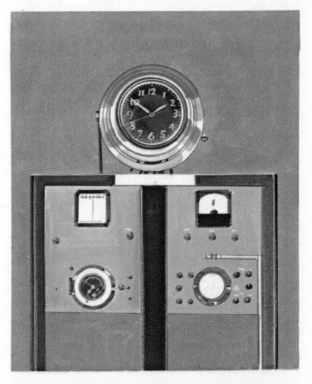

The first Ammonia Atomic Clock was built by the U.S. Bureau of Standards in 1949. The ammonia gas is in the wave guide that is wound around the face of the electric clock. The cabinet, seen only partly here, houses the oscillator and electronic circuits.

The controlling mechanism of the atomic clock and the celebrated pendulum of Galileo are separated by four centuries. The difference between the two pendulums in a way represents the growth of science. Although 16th century science did not depend on precise timekeeping devices, today such devices are absolutely necessary for scientific measurements.

Three dimensions — length, width and height — are

**Why is time frequently called the fourth dimension?**

ordinarily used to measure the size of objects. For example, we use length, width and height to measure the size of a solid block of wood.

The same three dimensions are used to measure the size, or volume, of space. Consider the space in a room. We can measure this space just as we measured the size of the wooden block — by noting the length, width and height.

The three dimensional method of measurement also allows us to describe the exact position of an object in space. Imagine that you are looking into a room. Hanging in the room is a ball attached to the ceiling by a piece of string. How can you describe the exact position of the ball in the room?

The position of the ball depends on its distance from three surfaces — in the same way that the size of an object and the size of space depend upon their three dimensions.

One of these surfaces can be either the floor or the ceiling. The other two surfaces can be any two connecting walls. For example, we can describe the exact position of the ball as three feet from the floor, seven feet from the north wall and five feet from the west wall.

Now suppose that the ball starts to swing. Because the ball is moving, its position constantly changes. It passes through a given position only at a given moment in time. Every new position of the ball is reached at a new moment in time.

Moving objects have a place in space and a place in time. To describe the position of a moving object, we measure its three dimensions in space and also observe the exact time at which we take the measurements.

The importance of time in describing the position of moving objects is one of the key ideas in the Theory of Relativity, formulated by Albert Einstein.

This great physicist regarded time as the fourth dimension. He treated time much the same as the dimensions of length, width and height. In his theory, length, width, height and time are so closely related that he refers to all of these dimensions with the single expression — space-time.

The earth turns, a heart beats, a liquid

**What does time tell us?**

flows, a crystal forms, a camera shutter opens and closes, a satellite is launched, a Geiger counter clicks, a gas expands, a fuel burns. How does time help describe these events?

We can answer this question only if we assign each event a beginning and an end. For example, when we measure the velocity of the earth's rotation (see Figures 1 and 2 on page 24), the first crossing of the sun over the meridian is called the beginning of our measurement and the second crossing the end.

Unlike the motion of the earth, which is continuous, the opening and closing of a camera shutter has a real beginning and a real end. Although the earth and the camera shutter have different types of motion, their velocities can be accurately measured.

Science defines the velocity of any moving object as the speed it travels between two places in a unit of time. Such terms as *miles per hour* and *feet per second* are familiar examples of this measurement of movement. It does not matter if the places in the definition are real or imaginary. All that is necessary when we want to time an event is that we know when to start and stop our measurement.

In everyday living, as in science, the great value of time is that it measures the interval between events. We cannot say that time causes something to happen, but only that it allows us to observe when it happens and for how long. This observation gives us understanding of duration, motion and change.

## Special Words in the Story of Time

A.M: the 12 hours before 12:00 noon. A.M. is an abbreviation of the Latin *ante meridiem,* meaning before noon.

●

ASTROLOGY: a false science which uses the position of the stars to tell fortunes and predict the future.

●

ASTRONOMY: the science which studies and explains the world of the heavens.

●

AXIS: the imaginary line passing through the earth on which the earth rotates. The various seasons are due to the angle of the earth's axis.

●

DAYLIGHT SAVING TIME: a time system which gives us more daylight hours. In areas that use Daylight Saving Time, clocks are set ahead 1 hour in the spring and back 1 hour in the fall.

●

EQUINOX: the time when the angle of the sun's rays crosses the equator, and day and night are of equal length everywhere in the world. The *vernal equinox* occurs about March 21 and the *autumnal equinox* about September 23.

●

FREQUENCY: the number of vibrations that anything makes during a period of 1 second.

●

GREGORIAN CALENDAR: the calendar, invented by Pope Gregory and a council of scientists in the 16th century, which we use today.

●

INTERNATIONAL DATE LINE: the 180° meridian of longitude. Each side of the Date Line has a different day. If it is Tuesday to the west of the Date Line, then it will be Monday to the east of the Date Line.

●

JULIAN CALENDAR: invented by the Roman emperor Julius Caeser under the guidance of the Greek philosopher Sosigenes. The Julian Calendar was used from 45 B.C. to 1582 A.D., when it was replaced by the Gregorian Calendar, which we use today.

LEAP YEAR: a year of 366 days. The extra day, February 29, is added once every four years to make up for the shortage in our calendar.

LIGHT YEAR: the distance that light, which has a velocity of 186,000 miles per second, travels in 1 year.

LOCAL TIME: mean solar time.

LUNAR: refers to the moon (from *luna,* the Latin word for moon).

MEAN SOLAR TIME: the time we use on our clocks and watches. It is adjusted to make up for the irregularities in the speed of the earth as it turns in orbit around the sun.

MERIDIANS OF LONGITUDE: imaginary circular lines which pass through the North and South Poles. In one hour the earth rotates 15°, or the equivalent of one meridian.

PENDULUM: a free swinging object, such as a weight hanging from a string, which has a back and forth motion.

P.M: the 12 hours after 12:00 noon. P.M. is an abbreviation of the Latin *post meridiem,* meaning after noon.

REVOLVE: the motion of a heavenly body as it follows a curved path (called an orbit) around another heavenly body. It takes the earth 1 year to revolve in its orbit around the sun.

ROTATE: to turn around as a wheel does. The earth rotates on its axis, producing day and night, while it revolves around the sun.

SIDEREAL TIME: also known as star time, is used by astronomers for special scientific work. It is the time required for the earth to complete one rotation with respect to a bright star.

SOLAR: refers to the sun (from *sol,* the Latin word for sun). Our *solar system* includes our sun and all heavenly bodies that revolve around it, such as the earth, the other planets, satellites, comets and meteors.

STANDARD TIME ZONES: 24 time zones extending around the earth. Each zone is contained in a 15° band of longitude. From one zone to the next the time differs by 1 hour.

VELOCITY: speed that an object travels in a unit of time along a known direction.

YEAR: 365¼ days or, to be exact, 365 days, 5 hours, 48 minutes and 46 seconds — the time it takes for the earth to travel around the sun.

ZODIAC: an imaginary band in the heavens separated into 12 equal distances by constellations (clusters of stars). The sun spends approximately 1 month in each of the 12 constellations on its yearly trip around the zodiac.